The Man I Met

How My Life Was Changed Forever

Paulett Coleby

ISBN 979-8-88685-270-7 (paperback)
ISBN 979-8-88685-271-4 (digital)

Christian Faith Publishing
832 Park Avenue
Meadville, PA 16335
www.christianfaithpublishing.com

Printed in the United States of America

Chapter 1

My name is Paulett Dixon–Coleby. I was born and raised in Riverside District, Hanover, Jamaica.

At the age of five, I went to Sis Tee Preschool. After I finished preschool, I went to Riverside Primary School. After that, I went to Grange Hill Secondary School and then Seventh-Day Adventist High School. I didn't get to graduate high school because my mom couldn't afford to pay school fees anymore.

My mother's name was Louise Jones Clarke. She was a single mother, raising eight children. I was the third child. My dad left my mother when she was pregnant with me. At this time my mom had three children with my dad when he left. My mom said she didn't know she was pregnant with me.

One day I asked my mom where my dad was. She said they had an argument and he tried to hit her. She told him, "If you plan to hit me, build your casket first," because she was going to kill him. She went on to tell him, "No man puts his hands on me and live." My mom said my dad started to sharpen a cutlass. My uncle came at that time and told him, "If you put your hands on my sister, you will be a dead man." So he packed up and left and never looked back. My mom said she would never allow any man to put his hands on her; he was not her father. When my dad left, he never came back, so my mom had to raise us on her own.

After I was born, my mom had four more children, so I was raised by my stepdad. He would always tell me he was my dad.

He always treated me the same way he treated his children. He never treated me less. He treated my brothers and sisters with love. He was a great father figure to me. But after my mom found out he was seeing another woman, they broke up. He had a lot of children with that woman.

As a child growing up, I always wanted to know who my father was. My brothers and I always felt empty. We had never seen our dad before. Life wasn't the way it should be for us.

My mother was a dressmaker. She would sew our school uniforms and some of our yard clothes.

My mom was also a farmer. She would get up early in the morning to go to her farm. My oldest brother would comb our hair and get us ready for school. He would fix our breakfast and make sure we ate before going off to school.

Sometimes my mother would take us with her to help her on the farm. I never liked the farm, but I would go anyway just to help my mom. All my mother's life she would just work. One thing I can say about my mom is she would never let us go to bed hungry. Our house always had food and was always clean. If we went to bed and didn't clean the kitchen, when my mom got home, she would wake us up to clean it. Everything had to be clean. She always said cleanliness is next to godliness. We knew what made her happy, so we would always make sure the house was cleaned before she got home from work.

Last but not least, my brothers had to keep the yard clean. She said the outside determines how the inside looks. If the outside is dirty, the inside is also dirty. So we had to sweep the yard and groom the plants.

I always heard my mother praying. She would always ask God to keep her alive so she could see her children pass the worst stage. She didn't want to die and leave us young. She wanted us to be able to take care of ourselves.

Growing up as I child, I would visit the kingdom hall with my grandmother. My mom would rarely visit because she was always working. My grandmother was such a great example to me. I used to say, "When I grow up, I want to be just like my grandmother." She loved everyone she met. Her love was unconditional. My grandmother was so humble and kind. I never heard her curse or swear. Everyone respected her. My grandmother left a path all her children and grandchildren could follow. She was always praying. She was a devoted woman of God. Sometimes I recall my grandmother cooking. She would always bring enough food to feed my mom, my sisters, my brothers, and me.

My grandmother was married, but her husband was not our grandfather. However, my mom depended on him financially. He would always make sure we got what we needed for school. They would go to the kingdom hall together. They would go from house to house to preach. My siblings and I looked up to them.

My mother's stepfather would try to molest me. He would tell me if I didn't let him touch me, he would not give my mother the money to buy my uniform and shoes for school. When my mother left the house, he would stop by to tell me he just needed to place his hands on me. I would run outside if I was inside the house, since we lived near the road and a lot of people would pass by. I would stay outside.

I was only a little girl in primary school. I remember it started when I was in fourth grade. I can't remember what exactly happened, but I remember one day I was cleaning the house and he came there and took off his clothes—he was naked. He told me he wanted to touch me. I told him no and I would scream, and I ran outside. I didn't tell my mother because my mother wouldn't believe me. I thought it would be rude if I talked. I was so afraid to tell my mom. He knew when to come by the house. When I would go by my grandma's house, he would ask me to give him a feel. I was so scared of him because he would always tell me I would not be going to school because he would not buy anything for me if I didn't allow him to do what he pleased. As a child growing up, I always loved school. So I couldn't tell my mom. I thought she would beat me. My mom was very strict. She always told us to be respectful to everyone we met. We were thought to be respectful, so we would never tell our mom certain stuff. It was hard for us to say things to our mom. We always felt as if it was out of order to say certain things, so we would keep them to ourselves.

Chapter 2

At the age of thirteen, a family friend came to our house. He told my mom he knew where my dad lived, so he could take us to see him. I and my brother were so excited. My mom told him she would have to think about it. It wasn't long before my mom decided.

My dad was living 150 miles away from where we were living. I was so excited to go and see my dad because as a child growing up, I always wondered how a dad could leave his children, never look back, and not even know if they were living or dead. It was both a scary and exciting moment for me. I really wanted to see my dad. I always saw other children with their fathers, so as a child it made me wonder, *What did I do? What did my mom do?*

I was so destroyed because of not knowing my dad. I would see my friends with their dads, and it made me feel empty inside. What can a child do to cause their dad to disappear and not even check or look back? My mom told us she made up her mind to send us to our dad's house, so we got dressed, me and my oldest brother. We went to see our dad. The ride was so long. We were tired and sleepy but very excited to see our dad. After hours and hours of traveling, we finally reached our dad's house.

Writing about it now, I remember how excited I and my brother were. When we got to our dad's house, he wasn't home. There was a lady with six children; they were all his children. She was so mad to see us because our father had never told her anything about us. She was very angry she told the gentleman who dropped us there that our dad didn't give her money and he had to bring us back because she couldn't take care of us. At that moment I and my brother knew we were in trouble. The gentleman left us there.

Our dad came home, and when he saw us, he was very upset. He didn't welcome us. We were so sad. We thought he would be excited to see us. We thought he would welcome us with open arms, but that was not what we received. When it was time for bed, I didn't know where I was going to sleep because it was a one-bedroom place with a front room. It was really small. Instead of six children, there were now eight children. I started to wonder where I would sleep, but my dad told me to sleep in the bed with him and his girlfriend. So I went to bed.

My dad slept in the front of the bed. I slept in the middle. When it was time for me to go to sleep, my dad started to put his hands in my panties. So I couldn't go to sleep, because as long as I kept twisting and turning, he would know that I was not sleeping. I couldn't wait for the sun to rise.

When daylight came, he left the house. As soon as he left, I went next door by my dad's cousin. I asked him if he could walk me to the shop. I needed to buy envelopes and writing papers. I wrote a letter to send to my mom. I knew it would take a while before my mom got my letter, maybe three days. Those three days felt like forever. I was so sad. I remember getting up one morning and I didn't see my brother. I asked my little brother where he was, and he told me he and my dad had a fight and my dad kicked him out. He was staying at his cousin's house. I told my little brother if I was there, he couldn't touch my brother. I didn't mean anything by it, but my little brother went and told my dad what I had said. My dad called me and started slapping me in my face and hitting me all over my head. I was so afraid, but I knew it would soon be over because once my mom got my letter, she would come running to get us. My brother couldn't come inside, or else he and my dad would fight. My dad wasn't a nice man. The man I waited my whole life to meet was nothing I dreamed of.

My mom had a sewing machine, and so did my dad's girlfriend. I would try to use her sewing machine to sew clothes for my dolls. One day I accidentally broke her sewing needle, and she was so upset. She said, "Wait until your dad gets home. I'm going to tell him, and he's going to beat you." I started to cry because I was so afraid at that moment.

However, by that time, our mom came to get us. I heard my mother say to my dad's girlfriend, "Did you see your children's father bring some children here?" She said yes. My mom said, "I come for my children." I was so happy. I went to get my brother, and we packed up our clothes and left.

It was a cold night, nearing the Christmas season. We were so hungry, and our mom brought us food. I was so happy I missed getting beaten by my dad for the sewing machine. We told her that we didn't want to ever leave her again. The ride was long, but we were happy to see our mom. She was all we had. She was the only person we could trust, as well as our grandmother.

I was so broken because it started to bother me a lot. I couldn't understand how a father could molest his own child. I wanted to know my dad because something was missing, but I regret the day I ever knew my dad. My whole life was messed up. I always wondered what I did to deserve such bad treatment. All I ever wanted was to be a daddy's girl. A dad should be trusted by his daughters, so I never understood why that had to happen to me. I always felt empty and worthless. Whom could I trust around me if I couldn't trust my own dad? I could only trust my mother and my grandmother.

As a child I started to feel as if every man wanted to use me or abuse my body in some way because if my dad did it, someone else would try. I still didn't tell my mom about her stepfather because I knew she would not believe me. I knew she would beat me. Now I knew my dad didn't like us, so we went home.

We were so happy to see our siblings. We were so happy to be together again. I went back to school. My mom so regretted sending us to our dad.

Chapter 3

I truly loved my family. I loved my siblings. I also loved my step-dad even though he and my mom were not together. Sometimes my mom would send us to our stepfather's house to pick up money for my younger siblings.

When I was fifteen, I remember one day my mom sent me to pick up money from my stepdad. On my way there, I saw one of the sons of my mom's best friend. He asked me if I needed a ride. Since it was about four to five miles, I took the ride. But when it was time to get off, he passed my stop and drove faster. I said to him, "Where are you taking me? I trusted you because your dad and my mother are good friends." He continued to drive. He went to pick up sugarcane, and then he passed my stop again and went to drop the sugarcane off at the factory. After he dropped off the sugarcane, he made a stop. I asked him, "Why are you stopping?" I said I had to get home since it was getting late and I was sure my mom was looking for me. I told him, "I know my mom. If she doesn't see me at a certain time, she will come looking for me." He said he was going to make sure I got home safe, but he did the complete opposite. He decided to rape me and drop me off at my stop. I didn't know what I was going to tell my mom. I trusted him because my mom knew him very well. He dropped me off. It was dark, and I had a couple of miles to get home. I told him I was going to tell my mom. He told me not to tell her anything.

When I got home, my mom asked where I was and said she was looking for me all over the place and could not find me. I told her what had happened. My mom was very angry with me. She beat me so bad. She said I shouldn't have taken a ride. I told her it was dark and the road was lonely, but my mom blamed me for everything. I got a lot of marks on my body from the beating. She left a lot of cuts and bruises. I explained to my mom that I trusted him because he knew us and she was good friends with his dad, but she still blamed me for taking a ride. I told her it was dark, and she knew I didn't like darkness. When it got dark, I would be inside since our community didn't have streetlights. My mom thought I should know better because of what my dad did, but because it was dark, all I wanted to do was get off the streets.

I truly loved my mom. I didn't hate her. She was trying to protect us. She was a single mother, and one thing I knew was she loved her children.

When it was morning, my mom took me to the house of the father of the guy who raped me. He was so mad about everything that happened. He begged my mom.

He said, "Please do not press any charges."

She told him, "You and I are friends, and I have children. I will not press charges."

He gave my mom money, and we went home. My mom told me not to take a ride from anyone. She said she didn't care who it was or if she knew them, because people are not who they say they are.

My friends knew what had happened. I ended up getting depression, and I had to take medication. I was scared to go back to school, so I stayed home for a year. After I went back to school, trying to fit in was hard, but *God had a plan for my life.* I thank God no one spoke about it when I went back to school, so I was not bullied. The problem was me. I knew what had happened, and I felt so empty.

I thank God for my siblings. We always played with one another, we comforted one another, and we were each other's best friend. At this point I still didn't tell my mom about her stepdad. I had so much bottled up inside. I never saw the boy anymore. He went to live in another country.

I always loved going to school as a child. Spelling, English, bioscience, and health science were my favorite subjects. I loved to walk to school alone. I never liked company, except my family members. I didn't want anyone else to know what I was going through.

Chapter 4

After I finished high school, my first job was in a hotel. I was working in the beauty salon. I loved to interact with the guests. After working there for a while, I started to find my true self. I started to feel beautiful again. I got my self-worth back. My boss loved me so much. No one at work knew what I was going through. I always went to work to do my job, smiling every day. I felt independent. My mom would not need help taking care of me anymore. I was now making my own money.

When I got paid, I would make sure to take out money for my mother first and keep the rest for me. My mother was a good mother. She loved us, and I loved her. I always wanted to work so that I could help my mom. I knew one day I would be working and taking care of my mother, so my first priority was to give my mom some money for herself, and then whatever was left was for me.

After I stopped working in the hotel, I went to rent a bar, and I and my cousin started our own business. My cousin was my best friend. She was always with me since I didn't want to be alone. Sometimes on weekends we would have parties. The hotel workers would support me. They would have a good time. Since I was close to the hotel, I always had customers coming by to have a good time. The bar was doing very well. I made sure my mom got something from whatever money I made. Now I could take care of myself and help my mom.

When I was nineteen years old, I met this guy. He would try to impress me by helping me financially. We became friends and started dating. Not very long after that, I became pregnant at twenty. When I got pregnant, I gave up the business. Then he started to cheat with different women. He started to abuse me. By this time I had already left my mom's house and lived with him. Whenever he beat me up, I would go back to my mother. Then he'd beg me to come back. I was going back and forth in the relationship. I ended up being fearful of him. He would threaten to burn my mother's house down, or he would threaten to shoot my mother.

I always said as a young lady I wanted to have all my children with one person and get married. I just wanted to settle down. I ended up having four beautiful children with him—three boys and one girl.

As time went on, things got worse. He would come home drunk and start an argument. I couldn't answer him. He would always say if I couldn't stay dumb, I could not stay in his house. Since I had children of my own now, I didn't want to stay by my mother's house anymore, so I preferred to stay there. But every time he would fight me, I would be by my mother's house to stay for a while. When I went there to stay, he would come and take my children. He knew I loved my children. He knew that if he took the children, I was going to come back to him.

When he started a fight and I said I was leaving, he would throw my clothes away in the pond. He would tear my clothes up. He would destroy my bags so I didn't have anything to pack my clothes in. He would fight me in front of my children, and I could only leave when he left for work.

I was so afraid of this man. I was terrified. I wanted to leave, but I didn't know how because he always threatened to kill me or my family. I would just run to someone else's house.

I remember one day he started a fight and I ran to my next-door neighbor. He came to my neighbor's house, kicked the door down, and dragged me out. He dragged me on the street straight home. My children would only watch, because what could they do? I knew one day I had to get away from this abusive relationship, or else I would end up dead.

One day we had a fight, and I ran to my girlfriend's house. He came there, dragged me out of the house, and punched me in my stomach. I remember blacking out. My head felt light. I felt so weak. He dragged me home. One of the neighbors said to him, "Why are you treating her like that? She's somebody's child." He cursed that neighbor out. So nobody came to stop him because everybody was afraid of him. But I knew within my heart I had to get out because if I didn't get out, this man was going to kill me.

He would abuse me for nothing. He would threaten me, so I had to stay there. He would threaten my family. I was scared for my family because my family didn't deserve to be killed by my kids' dad.

I remember one night he came home drunk. I and my kids were talking about him. We didn't know he was outside and was listening to our conversation. He came inside at about one o'clock in the morning. He locked us outside. We were outside in the dark. Only the smallest child was inside the house with him. I and my children were outside for hours, talking to each other. We were so afraid. All we could hear were dogs barking. It was so dark outside, but we stayed until he decided to let us in. My mom lived very far from us, requiring us to catch the bus. Since it was night and there was no bus, we just stayed outside until he let us in. It was almost daylight when he decided to let us in.

He would always tell me, "When I'm finished with you, no man is going to want you." When he started a fight, he would hit me in my head. One day I decided to ask his mom about how his dad treated her. She told me that he used to beat her every day. She said, "I'm even deaf in one of my ears now." I then realized what I was dealing with. She said my partner would watch his father beat her over and over. Now I knew where he got it from.

I wanted to leave so bad, but he knew where my mom lived, and I was scared for my children. I was fearful of him. I knew my best time to leave him was when he went to work.

One day we had a fight, and I went home to my mom's. When he got there, I was telling my mom about the fight we had, and he said to my mom that was not how it went. So I said to my mom, "Yes, Mom, that's how it went." He punched me in my head, and my mom reached to him and said, "No, don't do that." He pushed my mom, and she fell down. His sister was there and said to him, "No, no, you can't do that. You can't do that."

At that moment I realized this was time for me to leave. I had to leave since it was getting too serious now. My mom getting hurt didn't sit well with me. My mom was my everything, but I couldn't fight back because I knew he would kill me. But can I tell you this: *God had a plan for my life.* I didn't even know about the plan he had for me. I didn't know his plan for me was good and it was not evil and I didn't have to put up with what I was going through. But I knew even during my time of hurt, God was there protecting me, taking me through what I was going through. He was going through it with me.

That's why I am still alive because God had a plan for my life. This went on for about ten years. Within the ten years, I only had four children. God blessed me with four of the most beautiful children in the whole wide world. They're my joy even when I'm not feeling right. When I look at them, I feel joy. I feel peace. One thing I know for certain is whatever I went through, my kids were also going through it and they were very hurt. They couldn't do anything about it. They were helpless as they watched me suffer. My mom was always praying, asking God to help me so that I could leave him. But you see, God doesn't answer our prayers in our time all the time. His timing is right. I went through the abuse for ten years, and ten years was a long time for someone to be in an abusive relationship, but God kept me.

My partner didn't want me to work. I would go to work on my own risk. I knew my children needed to eat, so I went to work. On the weekend when I got paid, I went to shop and paid my bills. He would have so much alcohol on my bill, and I had to pay it because I didn't want a fight. I knew I had to leave. I knew I had to get out. I just didn't know how, but can I tell you this: *God had a plan for my life.*

Chapter 5

I would never forget the day my brother came. I was home when he came. He said there was a telegram by my mother's house for me. It was from my sister in the Bahamas, telling me to get my passport and myself ready because she wanted me to come to work. I cannot explain how I felt because I knew my life was about to change.

I was happy and sad at the same time because I wondered, *What about my children?* I knew if I went, my mom would take care of my children for me, but I'd have to send her money. I decided to go because I knew this was my way out. I knew it was now or never. My mom got my passport sorted out; she gave me the money to get it done. Now I had my passport, but I was still so worried about my children. However, I had to do it for us. Their dad said he would keep them. I really didn't want to leave them with him, but I knew I had no control. I didn't want him to fight my mom. I asked my mom to keep watch on my kids, and she said yes.

I asked a lady whom I knew in the area to cook for them and wash their clothes. My youngest child was only one year old at the time. My partner told me he would keep the children and I must send money to him and the lady who would do the cooking and washing, so I said okay. It was so sad to leave, but I knew my mother would be there to support and take care of my kids.

I went to the Bahamas and started to work. I sent money. Every paycheck I would send the money home for my children. My partner started to treat my children badly because he wanted me to come back. I would go home for Christmas and in the summertime.

I remember one day my mom said to me, "You cannot be coming home so often because you will not be able to save any money."

But my children were and still are my life. I was just trying to get a better life for my children.

My partner always said, "I don't care what you do to get the money as long as you send the money to me." I never knew I could be so afraid of one man. I was so fearful of him. I would have to send money, and I would have to be traveling back and forth all the time for my children.

I remember one day I went home to visit and he was cleaning the yard with the cutlass in his hand. He said to me he could not stand for me to go away another time. He didn't want me to leave this time. I was fearful because I thought he would kill me at that moment. I prayed right then, "Lord, if I leave, I am not coming back, because if I come back, he's going to kill me."

I went back to the Bahamas. I stayed there for three years. During that time he treated my children so bad. I was so stressed out. I found myself on medication to make me sleep because I could not sleep. Being in the Bahamas without my children was not easy. I remember visiting a doctor and he said to me, "I cannot give you any more sleeping pills because you need to go home to your children. You are addicted." He said the only thing that could fix my situation was to go back home to my children because I could not keep taking medication. I was becoming addicted.

I was working for this lady in the Bahamas, and she told me that I went home too often, so she couldn't do my papers anymore because it didn't make any sense. *But I knew God had a plan.*

After a while my mom took my children. When he knew I was coming home, he took the smallest one and kept him by his house. I remember one night I went by his gate and asked somebody to tell him to send my son so I could see him. He told the person to tell me to get away from his gate before he had to come out there. I was so scared, but I needed to see my baby because when I left him, he was only one year old. I had only seen him by going back and forth every year to visit. I spent two to three weeks with my children every visit. He knew this, so he took him because he was trying to be spiteful toward me. And he knew I was afraid of him because I knew what he was capable of doing.

I went back to the Bahamas without seeing my baby because he kept him away from me. I couldn't go by his house. I remember telling myself, "I'm going to stay in the Bahamas and get myself sorted out so I could get my children." No matter how much I tried, I couldn't find peace. I really missed my children.

When I went back to the Bahamas, I met this man. Not too long after meeting him, we got married. I got pregnant with my first child with him, so I didn't go home for three years. I didn't see my children in Jamaica for three years. The second I got my documents sorted out, I went home to visit my children. At this time they were living with my mother. My mother had to keep them because my former partner was treating them very bad. My children went through a lot because of the decision I had to make.

My mother was a good and very disciplined mother. She would discipline us even if we were right. She would also discipline my children even if they were right. My mother always taught us to be very respectful. She also taught my children to be very respectful. After I had my baby, it took me three years before I went back home to see my kids in Jamaica. When I went home, they were so happy to see me.

My oldest son said to me, "Mommy, I'm sorry you left my daddy."

I asked him, "Why are you sorry?"

He said, "Mommy, because now I would get to kill him."

I said, "No, I wouldn't want you to kill him and go to jail."

He said, "Mommy, he could never put his hands on you again because I would kill him. Mom, one thing I want you to do for me is take me to the Bahamas."

I spent a long time with my children before I went back to the Bahamas. My oldest son was the first one to come in the Bahamas. After my mom got sick and passed away, my daughter came also. She was the one who took my second son to the Bahamas. My youngest son was staying with my sister, and he would come to visit. He was living with my sister during my marriage. As time went on, life got a little better because I had my kids with me.

Chapter 6

After I got settled back in the Bahamas, my husband started to cheat. He would have ladies calling his phone. I remember at one point I picked up and answered his phone after it rang. It was a lady. He became extremely mad and punched me so hard in my ears. I couldn't hear for a long time. This was before my children came to live with me in the Bahamas. My ears were hurting for a long time, so I went to the doctor. He told me my eardrum was burst. It took a while to heal, but it did eventually.

He would get angry for no reason when he wanted to leave the house. I remember one day after I got pregnant with my third child with him, when I went to the clinic, his sweetheart was right there pregnant too. I had my baby on the 17th of February 2000, and she had her baby the 16th of February 2000. It was not easy for me. It was very rough. He was very abusive because that was the only way he could go and sleep out. He had to start a fight so he could leave.

I put up with the abuse for a while. I had three children with him, and so did his sweetheart. She was very bold. One day she came by our house to fight. My husband's sisters came out to beat her. They told her I didn't bother her and I was his wife. My husband was right there, but he didn't stop her. All he did was throw my stuff out in the road and tell me I had to leave. He told his sisters they must take care of me now because they got in his business. His sisters told him that all I did for him was be a good wife. His sweetheart didn't have respect; neither did he.

I left. It was very rough. After I left it was hard for me to get money from him for my kids. I ended up with depression all over again. I had to take medication for six months. I couldn't sleep in the night, but I knew I had to take care of my children. I had to work very hard to take care of my children. I had to find a babysitter to watch them. It wasn't easy.

At this time, I didn't have any rights to be in the Bahamas anymore. He would never do anything to get me my documents, so I was just living there until my spouse permit was up.

I remember one day I and my son, who just arrived in the Bahamas, had an argument. I called my husband to talk to my son. I was downstairs in the shop using the phone. I didn't know he went upstairs and pulled a knife on my son. My son held on to the knife out of fear and pulled the knife away. He almost lost his finger. He spent five days in the hospital. I thought he would act like a father to my son and just talk to him.

While I was in the shop downstairs, my daughter came with her mouth bleeding. She said she jumped from upstairs because she was scared after she saw the blood coming from my son's finger. When I went upstairs, I could not believe what I was saw. There was so much blood all over the house. My son was upset with me, and I was very upset with myself. I never ever thought he would hurt my son. He took advantage of me and my children because we were foreigners in his country. I went to the pay phone to call the police. My husband came with a gun and told me if I called any police on him, he would kill me, so I didn't call the police. I called his sister. She told me to not call the police since I didn't have any documents.

A couple of days after, he brought me a letter that he wrote to the Bahamas immigration. It was stating that he didn't hold any responsibilities for me and my children being in the Bahamas anymore. He told me to do myself a favor and go back home before I got sent home. This incident happened when my son and my daughter just came to the Bahamas from Jamaica.

I remember one night my husband and I had a quarrel. I remember him hitting me in my head and I passed out on the floor. When I came to, he said to me, "I almost killed you." I remember he poured water on my head after I came to. I was soaked in water. *But God had a plan*. I thank God for delivering me out of all the abuse.

My husband went away on a fishing trip and never came back. We separated after I got pregnant with our third child. We were separated when he died. He was with his new woman.

My kids were still very young when their dad died. I was a single mother with three kids. My kids from Jamaica were there with me also. My daughter from Jamaica finished high school, so she started to work, and so did my oldest son. So now I only had to take care of the smaller ones.

When my husband died, he still didn't put in for my papers, but can I tell you *God had a plan*. One day I applied for permanent residency, and the minister called me and told me I was entitled for citizenship because I was living in the Bahamas long enough. I was so happy. God had blessed me with my documents not just to reside but to stay.

Chapter 7

A few years after my husband died, I met this gentleman. We started dating, which went on for eight years. He was very good to my children. Before they left for school, he would make certain my children had food and lunch money. He would make sure they had uniforms. Also, he was very good and helpful to me. He would make sure I always had money to take care of the children.

One night I went to the Adventist crusade. As I started worshipping, the Holy Spirit started to convict me. They asked if anyone wanted to get baptized. I said I did. I needed to get baptized, so I went in the pool and got baptized.

I was still with the gentleman, but I knew it was wrong. It was like something had shifted in me. I remember one night he picked me up to go by his house. I was sitting in his truck, and I said to him, "I cannot do this anymore." He asked why. I said I felt dirty, I felt nasty, and I felt like a prostitute. Something wasn't right. The Holy Spirit, the spirit of the true and living God, was convicting me. The gentleman turned to me and said, "I don't want to force you to go by my house." He asked what happened, and I said I just wanted to go and serve the Lord. Then he said, "Anything for God. I wouldn't stop you." He released me and let me go that very moment. That was about seven years ago. He never looked back, and I never looked back either. I respect that man so much because he did not fight with me. He was so humble, so I knew it was God's plan.

After I got baptized, I kept saying to the Lord, "Father, you said you will take care of me. You are my Provider, and I need you to show me that you are my Provider. I need to depend on you. I don't want to live this life anymore. I want to live for you." And my prayer was answered. Thank God for the Holy Spirit. Thank God for the spirit of truth because when the spirit of truth came, I could never live a life of lies anymore.

I have to live a life of truth because you see, the spirit of truth teaches truth and the spirit of lies teaches lies. Now, the spirit of truth came and takes full control of my life. My life was changed that very night. You see, sometimes we just want an encounter with God. One encounter will change our lives forever.

All I want to do is to serve God. I started to have a hunger and a thirst like I cannot get enough. I would go to church every time the church door is open. I would worship God in spirit and in truth and in the very beauty of holiness. Nothing in this world pleases me anymore. All I want is Jesus. All I want to do is serve God. All I want is to run after him, all I want is to chase after him, and all I want is more of him. I couldn't get enough.

You see, I didn't know that there was a man who could change my life forever. I heard about him. I read about him, but I never had an encounter with him. I knew he saved my life over and over. I knew I could have died during the abuse. I knew there was a time when I think I wouldn't make it, but I never had a real encounter with a man called Jesus. You see, God gave us a choice to serve him. I made the wrong choices at first. I was selfish. I believed in all the lies Satan was telling me. My spiritual eyes were blinded. My spiritual ears were deaf until the Holy Spirit came. I was living in sin, but when I had an encounter with the man named Jesus, my whole life was changed forever and ever.

Chapter 8

Jesus is the man I met who changed my life forever. Jesus is the one who takes away every abuse, every curse, and every heartache. Jesus is the one who gave me peace. You see, the world cannot give me peace. True peace comes from God.

One night I dreamt that I was flying. I was flying over water. The water was so pretty I had to dip myself in it. I started to fly again. Then in the dream, I found my hands tied in an outside toilet. I heard gunshots. I said I had to get out of this toilet, but my hands were tied in the dream. Eventually, I found a fish scraper, so I was able to cut the cord off my hands. I woke up out of the dream after I escaped out of the outside toilet.

The very next morning, I was on my way for a job interview. My phone rang, and it was my daughter-in-law. She said my son got shot in his stomach three times. He was in surgery for seven hours. She was not sure if he was going to live. But you see, faith stepped in. I started to pray. I went back home, went in the house, and started to cry out to the Lord. I said, "Lord, if you save my son, I will give you my life forever. I will serve you forever and ever." That was a day my faith was high in God. After praying in the house, I went outside and looked up to heaven. I said, "Lord, if you save my son, I will serve you forever." That very day faith kicked in. My faith was so high in God there was no doubt in my heart my son was going to live. No one could have told me otherwise. All I was thinking about was asking God to save my son's life. I said, "Lord, I believe you could do it. I know you could do it, and I am standing on faith."

After the surgery was over, my daughter-in-law called me. She said he lost a piece of his liver and one kidney, so now he was living with one kidney and a piece of liver. I told the Lord I would tell the world how great he was. I went on Facebook and posted how great God was. I promised him. I made a vow to God that I would serve him until I die. With one kidney and a piece of his liver, my son was living a healthy life—all because of faith. Ever since that day, my faith in God has been elevated to a whole new level. There is no more doubt in my heart because I know he could do it. God is a promise keeper.

God had prepared me with that vision. In the vision the water was clear, and I know clear water is a good dream. God was showing me exactly what my son was going through. I bore my son's burden in that dream, and there is no doubt in my mind that it is only God who saved him. I was prepared for what happened to my son. My son's story changed my whole life. I look at life differently now. My son's story made me the woman I am today, a faith walker in Christ.

You see, we have to learn to trust Christ in the good times and in the bad times. He's the same yesterday, today, and forevermore. God never changes. Thank God for what happened to my son. Thank God for that day. Because of that day, I am a firm believer, a devoted woman of God, on a mission for my Father in heaven.

I can stand up and tell the world to trust God in the midst of every circumstance or situation. He's faithful if we believe. I believe that my God could change any situation that I go through. And I could tell the world if they trust him, they, too, could go through any situation because he is going through it with them. I wouldn't trade that day for anything. All we need is an encounter with Jesus, and our life will never be the same. Out of my son's story, God gets the glory.

As you will come to see, God said in Mark 11:23 (KJV), "For verily I say un unto you, That whosoever shall say unto this mountain be thou removed and be thou cast into the sea and shall not doubt in his heart but shall believe that those things which he saith shall come to pass, he shall have whatsoever he saith."

God's Word cannot lie. He said so, and it is so. As God said in Matthew 24:46 (KJV), "Blessed is that servant, whom his Lord when he cometh shall find so doing."

God said in his Word in Matthew 6:33 (KJV), "But seek ye first the Kingdom of God and his righteousness and all these things will be added to you."

Now I knew that it was time to stop running from God. Now I knew it was time to put faith into action. Now I knew it was time to seek first the kingdom of God and all his righteousness. My faith is so strong in God now. I depend on God to lead me and direct me in every area of my life.

I found a man who loves me, a man who believes in me. I found a man who gives me peace. I found a man who is a great provider. I found a man who is a protector who would protect not just me but my whole family. I found a man who is never too busy for me. I found a man who tells me in Psalm 34:15 (NIV), "The eyes of the Lord are on the righteous, and his ears are attentive to their cry."

I know I have someone who watches over me. I know I have someone who does not sleep or slumber. Psalm 121:3–4 (KJV) says, "He will not suffer thy foot to be moved…he that keepeth Israel will never slumber nor sleep."

I found a man whom I am chasing after now. I found a man I cannot get enough of. I would get up at three or four in the morning to lie on my face before him. I still can't get enough of him.

I would fast and pray. Every time the church door opens, I would be in church. I wouldn't miss a prayer meeting. I was chasing after God, and I am still running after God.

Chapter 9

One day I started feeling sick. I was sick for a whole year. The doctor couldn't point out what was happening to me. Some said it was menopause. Some said I might be eating too much fish. I didn't know what was happening to me. I couldn't sleep in the night. In the night I would pray for daylight, and in the day I would pray for night to come down so I could get some rest. I was praying that I would be healed. I was placed on medication for depression, but every day my prayer would be "Though they slay me like Job, I will trust the Lord. I would never give up on my God."

God was and still is all I have. He is my source. I knew only him could heal me. I knew my healing was in God, so even though I was going through it, I still was trusting my God. I knew one day he was going to heal me. I didn't know when, but I knew he was going to do it. I always remembered Psalm 34:19 where God said, "Many are the afflictions of the righteous but the Lord delivereth them out of them all." I was standing on the Word of God.

I got so weak one day a friend of mine invited me to a church. I called the church and asked for prayer. The secretary told me I had to make an appointment and bring $500 for prayer. I told her I didn't have that kind of money. So she said to come to the healing service on Friday night at eleven and if the prophetess located me, she would pray for me. I went with the lady who invited me. There, she asked me what I did and why I was not healing. I said to her I didn't do anything and I had to wait on God's timing. You see, I was just going through a process. Something wasn't right in my spirit. In that church my spirit was very upset. The atmosphere didn't feel right.

A doctor placed me on Prozac for a little while, but it had too many side effects. Then he changed my medication to Paxil. It wasn't helping me, and I kept going to different doctors. One of the doctors placed me on Xanax. That was the worst one. It made me very sick. I lost a lot of weight, but I was able to sleep in the night. The side effects were terrible.

I remember one day after taking Xanax I heard a voice telling me to take all the pills. I called my doctor immediately, and he told me not to take any more; it was the side effect. I called my niece at work and told her what was happening, and she told me to come to spend the day with her at work. I went by her work, and we talked. I started to feel a little better.

The doctor took me off Xanax. I told the doctor to put me on Zoloft, so he said he would. I told him after I and my husband separated, I ended up with depression and was placed on Zoloft. He placed me on Zoloft, and it worked. So he changed the medication and placed me on Zoloft. The first two weeks I started to feel so much better. I started to feel like myself again. I was so happy. My prayer was "Lord, I know you could do it. I will not give up on you. I've proved to you over and over. You are the same God yesterday, today, and forevermore."

I didn't have to pay $500 for prayer. My God is a healer. Healing comes from God, not man.

I remember one day while taking Xanax my son called me.

He said, "Mom, what are you taking?"

I replied, "Xanax."

He said, "Mom, please, you need to get off them as soon as possible. They are not good for you."

But *God had a plan*.

Xanax was so addicting. It made me get some sleep in the night, but the side effects were so terrible. And what I was going through was a spiritual battle, not a physical one. I would get up in the daytime. I would read my Bible. I would pray. I would write down scriptures. I would go to church as soon as the church door was opened. I would go to prayer meetings. I wouldn't miss church. I would fast. I would sing. Even with what I was going through, I still kept my mind on Christ.

I remember one night I went to a church service and the spirit of God came upon me so strong that I hugged a church sister of mine and I couldn't stop embracing her. She told me that there was fire of God on me. Then she said, "You are anointed, and I could feel the fire coming from you." Just then I knew that my testing was worth it.

Sometimes the process takes a long while, but it is always worth it. I stopped watching television at home. I took the television out of my bedroom. Instead, I chose to spend quality time in God's Word and in the presence of a holy and righteous God. My desire is to serve God. All I want is God.

God started to speak to me in dreams, and at times, he would give me visions. By the time I got out of the vision, he would interpret it to me. I didn't have to ask anyone what my dreams meant, because every time the Lord gave me a dream or a vision, he would then interpret it to me. At the same time, he would wake me up early in the morning to pray. He said in Joel 2:28 (KJV), "And it shall come to pass afterward, that I will pour my spirit on all flesh, your sons and your daughters shall prophecy, your old men shall dream dreams, your young men shall see visions."

I remember I was in prayer and the Lord told me to give away the clothes in my closet. I had to ask him again. I said, "Lord, is this you talking?" I heard the voice again. It started to rest heavy in my spirit, so I knew it was the Lord speaking to me. I knew there were a lot of young people in our church who needed clothes, so I decided to pack my clothes in two big black garbage bags. I called my pastor's wife to pick up the clothes. I left six outfits in my closet. I was standing on faith. I said, "Lord, you told me to give away those clothes, and I know you have better for me." I started to wear the outfits I had left in my closet; they were church clothes. Three months passed, and I said, "Lord, I am tired of wearing these clothes over and over to church. You promised me." One night I went to church, and the prophetess called me up.

She said to me, "I see God giving you a new wardrobe."
I said, "Wow."
She said, "Yes, because you are faithful."
So I knew it was the Lord who spoke to her.

One day my best friend called me. She said there was a lady having a sale on clothes and she wanted both of us to go. She needed some church clothes herself. We made the appointment and went to buy the clothes. When we got there, there must have been over thirty different dresses, and all the dresses were in my size, but there was none at all to fit my friend. They were just far too big for her. I told the lady I would buy all the dresses. She said the dresses cost over $100 each but she would give them to me for $20 each, and I could not believe it. Even with that offer, I didn't have enough money to pay for everything, so I told her I would make a down payment on the dresses and pick them up later. To this she said okay. She also said, "I cannot let my sister know I sold these dresses so cheap because she would be very upset with me, so I'm going to pack them and put them aside for you to pick them up later." When I got back home, the Holy Spirit quickened me and said, "I told you I was going to bless you with better." I went back in the evening to pick up the dresses from the lady. She said to me, "There is something about you. I can't tell what it is, but I couldn't give you the dresses for more than $20 each." I started to testify and tell her how the Lord told me to give away everything that I had in my closet and he was going to bless me with better. Then I prayed with her. So now I know that I can hold on to the promises of God. If he said so, I believe it. Those dresses were so much better than the ones I gave away.

I started to go to sales, and I would buy clothes to give to the church. I would stock up on things so if someone in the church needed something, I would have enough to share. If someone moved in a new apartment and they needed stuff, I would always have stuff to share because now I know the God I serve will never leave me nor forsake me.

I would always want to have enough to share. There is a blessing in giving. I would always sacrifice to get enough stuff to share. I have so many testimonies.

One night I went to a crusade, and the prophet told me, "You are going to the bank, and you are going to find money on your account. That money is yours. Take it off because the Lord is going to bless you." And I believed the prophet.

When I was sick, I remember owing my landlord $2,000, and I said to my daughter I would like to pay my landlord at least $1,000. I was praying about it. I said to the Lord I had to pay my landlord at least $1,000. After my husband passed away, I started to get some money for my children and myself from the government. I sent my daughter to the bank. I said, "Go to the bank and take the money off my account that the government put there for us."

When my daughter went to the bank, she called me from the bank and said, "Mommy, instead of $400, on your account is $1,000 and some change."

I said to her, "You're not telling the truth."

She said, "Yes, Mommy, it's $1,000 and some change."

So I asked, "Can you get the $1,000 off?"

She said yes and came home with the money. I was able to give my landlord $1,000. I was worrying about it at first, but there was a lady from the church who said, "No, you cannot worry because the prophet already told you the Lord is going to bless you and you will find money on your account." I was able to pay my landlord, just what I asked the Lord for. God is an awesome God, if we only trust him and believe in him. When a man or a woman of God speaks over my life, I hold on to the word with faith. If it's not registered in my spirit, I will not hold on to it. Proverbs 18:21 (KJV) tells us, "Death and life are in the power of the tongue; and they that love it shall eat the fruit thereof."

God knows our needs before we ask. He knows what we need because he is our Creator. Ephesians 3:20 (KJV) says, "Now unto him that is able to do exceedingly abundantly above all that we ask or think according to the power that worketh in us."

I know I can trust God. He is the same God yesterday and forevermore. God doesn't change.

I had to learn to trust God in every area of my life. My God never fails me. Even in my sinful life, he kept me. God could have allowed the enemy to take me in my sinful life, but he had a plan for my life. When God has a plan for your life, no one could stop the plan of God for your life.

He said in Isaiah 40:22 (NIV), "He sits enthroned above the circle of the earth and its people are like grasshopper. He stretches out the heavens like a canopy and spreads them out like a tent to live in." So I know I can trust God. He's the same God today and forevermore. I don't care how the situation looks. I don't care how it feels. We can still trust God. God is our ultimate source.

After all the sickness I had been through, *God had a plan* for my life. After all the pain, after all the hurt, after all the abuse, after all the molestation, *God had a plan* for my life. God's plan and God's timing are the best for my life. Jeremiah 29:11 (NIV) says, "For I know the plans I have for you, declares the Lord, plans to prosper you and not to harm you, plans to give you a hope and a future." God's plan for our life is best.

All I went through in God's timing was right for my life. In the one year of sickness I went through, God had made me a new person. I was anointed. God started to use me in the healing ministry. I was ordained to be a minister by my bishop.

One day I was asking God to lead me to the right church. He spoke to me right in my garden. He said he gave me the fivefold ministry. I have a close relationship with God. I don't want to do anything that the Holy Spirit doesn't direct me to do. When I go to church, I start to feel the anointing so strong I would be worshipping and can't keep still. I would be sitting down while the pastor is preaching and would be swaying from left to right. When I see where God brought me from, I couldn't keep still. I will go to church, and people will be sitting down worshipping God. But if I stay in the church long enough, people will join me and start moving up and down.

One day I was missing from church. My church sister told me that they asked her where the lady who ran up and down in church was. They said my presence was missing.

The Lord used me mightily one day. One night my daughter went out. It was her birthday. When she got back home, she went to sleep. Her son's dad came early in the morning by our house. I didn't know he and my daughter had an argument the night before and my daughter took his car keys, so when he came to the house, I let him in. He went into her room and took his car keys. I didn't know he took her phone the night before and that was why she took his car keys. After he took the keys, my daughter got up out of her sleep. She said to me he had her phone. She ran after him. He sped off in his car, and she fell on the floor and passed out. She was unconscious, so I started to pray. My son said, "Mommy, you can't be seeing a girl dying and praying." I said to him Jesus first, doctor second. Calling the ambulance was my last resort. I learned to trust in Jesus. My son and my other daughter were panicking, but I learned to trust in Jesus. My son called the ambulance, but it took very long. I did not call my neighbor. I did not call my friends. I was calling on Dr. Jesus all along. The ambulance came. The emergency responder started to press her chest doing CPR very hard until her eyes rolled. And I was still praying. He pressed her chest so hard until I heard her start groaning. They put her in the ambulance and took her to the hospital. On the way to the hospital, I was still praying. When we got to the hospital, after the other gentleman strolled her in, one of the emergency responders said to me, "You have a healing gift. I listened to you praying, and the spirit told me you have a healing gift." I said to him it was prophesied over my life before, and he said to me, "I am a pastor. I have a church in Jamaica."

After my daughter woke up, she asked me how she got there, and I told her what had happened. She got up, said to the doctor she was going home, and walked outside the hospital.

I asked her, Aren't you going to wait?"

She said, "No, Mommy, you already prayed for me. And I believe in your prayers."

The doctor came outside and said to her, "You cannot leave unless you sign yourself out because if anything happens to you, we are not responsible."

She went back in the hospital and signed herself out. We went home, and she was fine. Nothing ever happened to her from that day.

God is our ultimate source. We only need to trust him. I believe in his Word. I have faith in his Word, and I trust him.

My neighbors didn't know what happened until this day. I never told anyone but Dr. Jesus.

One time I went to a church service, and the prophetess prophesied to me.

She said, "The Lord gave you a healing gift. The Lord gives you dreams. He gives you visions, and he interprets them to you."

I said, "Yes, ma'am, he does."

She said, "I see you pray for people and they are healed."

She was only confirming what other prophets spoke to me.

God is so good. The emergency responders spoke to me and said that my daughter could have died because she suddenly got up out of her sleep and ran outside and the blood rushed to her head. She could have died right there and then. Also, she was drinking alcohol the night before at the party.

We can trust in God. We can always lean on him.

Romans 12:3 (KJV) says, "For I say through the grace given unto me to every man that is among you not to think of himself more highly than he ought to think but to think of yourselves soberly according as God hath dealt to every man the measure of faith."

My daughter's faith level was high, so God moved on her behalf. My daughter's trust was in God, not in man. We respect our doctors, but we know there is a higher power who has to instruct our doctors.

God is the one who gives them wisdom, knowledge, and understanding. No man operates without God. Isaiah 53:1 (KJV) says, "Who hath believed our report? And to whom is the arm of the Lord revealed?"

Hebrews 12:1–2 (KJV) says, "Wherefore seeing we also are compassed about with so great a cloud of witnesses, let us lay aside every weight, and the sin which doth so easily beset us, and let us run with patience the race that is set before us, looking unto Jesus the author and finisher of our faith; who for the joy that was set before him endured the cross, despising the shame, and is set down at the right hand of the throne of God." We have to understand that we will go through rough times in life but only for our season. No one situation lasts forever.

Psalm 34:19 (KJV) says, "Many are the afflictions of the righteous but the Lord delivers him out of them all." So even though we go through situations, we will only go through them because God will deliver us out of them all. He said *all*, not some. We have to believe.

After I found out that God was using me with the gift of healing, I started to pray for people. I also had a ministry on my phone where I would send messages out every day so people would call me and ask me to pray with them. I would pray for their healing. I would encourage them. I would pray for their jobs.

I use the gift that God has placed in me. I see miracles, signs, and wonders happen. I see God move on my behalf a lot of times. The Holy Spirit dwells in me. I could forgive easily. I have more peace, more joy. When I pray, I always ask God for wisdom, knowledge, and understanding. I always ask God to fill me up. When I pray, I ask God to give me a hunger for him. I found myself running after God. I cannot get enough of God.

I always have a hunger; I always need more. I understand that in God there is a deeper depth, so I just don't want to get comfortable. I always desire to go higher in God, so I would spend time in the Word. I want to have a close relationship with him. Nothing else matters. All I want to do is to be in the presence of God. I love to bask in his presence. Psalm 16:11 (NIV) says, "You make known to me the path of life; you will find me with joy in your presence, with eternal pleasure at your right hand." I am not using my own strength anymore.

I depend on God's direction. It's not about me anymore; it's all about Jesus. I learned to depend on God in every area of my life because he tells me so in his Word. Psalm 37:23–25 (NIV) says, "The Lord makes firm the steps of the one who delights in him; though he may stumble, he will not fall, for the Lord upholds him with his hand. I was young and now I am old, yet I have never seen the righteous forsaken or their children begging bread."

Now my steps are ordered by the Lord. I will not go anywhere I shouldn't go. I would not do the things that are not of God. I am not perfect, but every day I strive for perfection.

My life was changed forever. I am a new person in Christ Jesus. God's Word cannot lie. If he said so, I believe it. Numbers 23:19 (KJV) tells us, "God is not a man that he should lie nor a son of man that he should repent. Hath he said and shall he not do? Or hath he spoken and shall he not make it good?"

Once God said it, I have to believe it. His promises are a yes and amen.

We should not doubt God. I've come to a place in my life where it's all about God. What he says I will do. Wherever he leads me, I will follow.

Chapter 10

My daughter was a vibrant child and never got sick. However, five months after she had her own daughter at age sixteen, her health changed. I remember one day she went to the shop and after she got back home she fell on the floor with a seizure. She was shaking. At that time I was not baptized yet. I didn't have a relationship with God. The seizures went on for years. She would get jobs, but she'd always leave them. The seizures got so bad sometimes she would fall and hit her head. I believe the seizures took over her life all because I didn't meet Jesus. After I got saved and started praying for her, the seizures went away. They never came back. Because when God fixes it, it is well-fixed.

I know God is a healer. I've proved it over and over. I am blessed to have the opportunity to tell the world about my Jesus—my Deliverer, my Savior, my soon-coming King. His name is Jesus Christ, our Lord and Savior. He saved me. *Jesus is the man I met who changed my life forever*. I have a testimony. He saved me. Hallelujah! God said in Psalm 84:11 (KJV), "For the Lord God is a sun and shield: the Lord will give grace and glory: no good thing will he withhold from them that walk up rightly." So I know once I do the things that he called me to do, I will be okay.

I had to learn to trust God. My faith in God is rooted and grounded. In Psalm 119:105 it is said, "Your word is a lamp to guide my feet and light for my path." So I have to be rooted and grounded. I stand on God's Word because that's where I find peace in the midst of the storm. As a child of God, the Holy Spirit always quickens me and lets me know where I am going wrong. If I put on a dress that is not pleasing to God, the Holy Spirit will let me know something is not right with the dress. If I say something to someone and I am not aware it's not pleasing, the Holy Spirit will tell me to go and apologize.

I love the Holy Spirit because the Bible said in John 18:13 (NIV), "But when he the spirit of truth comes, he will guide you into all the truth; he will not speak on his own; he will speak only what he hears and he will tell you what is yet to come." I thank God for the Holy Spirit, the true spirit of the Almighty God. We have to listen to the voice of the Holy Spirit. The Bible said in Romans 8:14, "For as many as are led by the spirit of God, these are sons of God."

As I study God's Word and see his promises toward us, it makes me stronger in faith. It makes me trust God more. When I look at his creation and see his hand at work, I have no other choice but to trust him. I look at the ocean and see how God created the sea. He tells the water where to stop. Psalm 33:7 tells us, "He gathered the waters of the sea together as a heap: he layeth up the depth in storehouses."

With the things I see God do in my life, I have no other choice but to worship him in spirit and in truth and in the very beauty of holiness.

I was walking to work one day, and my son called me. He said, "Mommy, you need to come home right now." I asked him what happened, and he told me he and another boy got into an argument and the other took up a Vita Malt bottle to hit him. The boy apparently called his mother and told his mom that my son pulled a gun on him. I knew my son didn't have a gun, but eventually his mom called me at my work and said she was going to the police because my son pulled a gun on her son. I knew that was a lie because the Holy Spirit had already quickened me, so I told her my son didn't have a gun. She began arguing and cursing on the phone.

She said, "I am going to the police station."

I asked her, "What type of gun is it?" She told me what type of gun it was, and I knew she was lying. I said to her, "I will meet you in the police station."

I left work, I started to pray, and I said to God, "Holy Spirit, go before me and lock that woman up and arrest her because I know and you know she's not speaking the truth. My son doesn't have a gun." I left work in the spirit and headed straight to the police station with my son. When we reached the police station, the woman was sitting inside. The police asked us to go in the back with him. The policeman started to sing a gospel song, and I was singing with him also.

When we got in the room, the police officer asked her, "What is the problem?"

She said, "My son pulled a Vita Malt bottle on her son, and I want it to stop right now. I don't want them to continue to fight."

I was stunned. I knew she was lying, but the Holy Spirit went and dealt with her so she had to speak the truth. After the police officer talked to my son and her son, I told the police officer I was going to pray. I started to pray.

The police officer said to my son, "Do you know your mother is a praying woman?"

My son said, "Yes, sir."

I said to my son, "You and him have to make peace."

So my son and her son made peace. They hugged and apologized to each other. After everything was over, the mother said to me it was nice meeting me. We exchanged phone numbers, and we started talking on the phone. I encouraged her, and she said she thanked God for what happened. She was happy of the outcome. We became friends, and we started to pray together on the phone in the morning time. We learned to trust God in every situation that we go through. He will make a way out of no way. God told me so in his Word in Mark 9:23: "Jesus said to him, 'If you can believe, all things are possible for the one who believes.'"

As a child growing up, my mom would say to me, "Belief kills, and belief cures." We have to learn to trust God. During my walk with God, I never doubted him. I have to trust him in any situation I go through. I am a faith walker in Christ. He always shows up in every area of my life. I always remember my mom saying, "If he shows up today, he will show up tomorrow." God never changes. He told us in his Word to trust him, so I learned to trust God. Even when I don't see a way, I know he will make a way out of no way. Whatever he said in his Word, the Holy Bible, I believe.

One morning I was in prayer. I was praying to the Lord, "I want you to save my children. Father God, please save my children." One morning I was lying down and was talking to him in my spirit. He said to me, "I'm going to save your children." That was confirmation for me. Two of my children were already saved. That following month my daughter got saved.

We only have to ask God and believe that he will do it. God is always on time. He never lies. I know God is in control. Everyone should have a personal relationship with God. He said in John 10:27–28, "My sheep hear my voice. I know them and they will follow me and I give unto them eternal life and they shall never perish; neither shall any man pluck them out of my hands."

I remember walking to work one morning and the spirit of God spoke to me. He said, "You are my remnant." When we have a close relationship with God, we don't need anyone to tell us what God says about us and who God says we are in him because God speaks to us himself."

I remember another day I was on my way to work and the spirit of the Lord spoke to me. He said, "Your name changed. Your name changed to Prophetess Deborah. Many are going to rise up against you. But remember when you speak, it is not you who are speaking; it is the spirit of the living God speaking through you, and no one can hurt the spirit of the living God." That very moment a boldness came over me. I never have any fear to deliver God's Word anymore.

All I want to do is to tell people about *the man named Jesus.* I never knew that there was so much peace in serving God. I can never get enough. I started to hear conversations even if I am not around them. I remember lying on my bed and some of the church members were talking about the pastor. I asked the ladies whom I heard in the spirit, and they admitted they said those very same words. I started hearing people talking about me over and over. I would pray about things, and the Lord would speak to me. Sometime he will send someone to me with a word of confirmation. Sometimes he will send me a word. I ask, and he answers. My relationship with God is all that matters.

I remember I was walking from work and the spirit said to me, "Cover your head when you are coming in my presence to reverence me." I remember seeing my grandmother. She always had her head covered. She would never pray without her head covered. Before I started going to church, I would only wear pants. I never really liked dresses, but after I built a relationship with God, a lot of things changed.

One day I started getting dressed for work. When it was time to put my pants on, it didn't feel good anymore, so I stopped wearing pants when I went out. I would wear sweatpants in my garden and to walk around the park, but I wouldn't wear pants in the house of God. I am not against ladies wearing pants because God deals with everybody in his own way.

I remember one time I couldn't wait to get out of bed, eat, and get ready to watch my favorite TV show. However, I was remined my relationship with God was all that mattered. So I took the TV out of my bedroom. I don't watch TV anymore. I just want to spend time with God, doing the things he called me to do.

It's so sweet to trust in Jesus, just to take him at his Word, just to lean upon his promise. People have said to me a couple times, "Remember you are still on planet earth. Don't try to be so holy." But they don't know the cost of the oil. I remember a lot of people who used to say to me, "Remember that you are a sinner." We cannot worry about what people say about us. We have to pray for them. I love them anyway. People will never understand. People will never know the time you spend in the presence of God. People will never know your sacrifice doing the things of God.

Sometimes God will wake me up in the night, and he will drop someone in my spirit to pray for them. We can't worry about what people say when we know we are doing what we know is best to serve Christ.

One day my daughter came to me, and she said, "Mommy, I met this lady who is paralyzed for four-and-a-half years. I need you to go and pray with this lady." I told her, yes, I would. I asked my other daughter to go with me to the woman's house. We went there and prayed for her. A couple days after, my daughter, whom I brought along with me to pray, said to me, "Mommy, I dreamed about the lady in her garden. Why is she not walking yet?" My daughter always had faith. I told my daughter it was in God's timing. So one day as I was walking to work, the spirit of God told me to call her and pray with her and tell her she was going to walk.

At that moment a voice said to me, "How can you tell her she's going to walk? Are you sure?"

I responded, "Yes, if God said so, it will surely be so."

This lady was living in the Bahamas, but she went back to Jamaica for medical treatment. When I called her phone, she was not answering. I called her son who lived in Jamaica. I didn't get him either, but I continued to call her phone. I couldn't stop calling. It was pressing on me so hard. There was no answer, so I left a message. I told her in the message that the Lord said she was going to walk and the Lord gave me a scripture: one for me and one for her. It was about three in the afternoon. I needed to eat since I didn't eat in the morning. I was very hungry. I told her in the message, "I am on a fast, and I need to pray for you before I eat any food." I also told her to please call me. I knew it was the spirit of God. Past three, she called back. She said, "Woman of God, I just told God this morning that I was not hearing from him. Then God sent you to call and message me, so I know it is from the Lord." I prayed with her over the phone. I told her the Lord said she was going to walk. My faith was so high. I believe God said it and God was going to do it because he does it over and over and over and over.

I prayed with her. I gave her the scripture that the Lord gave me to give her. A couple of days after, she called me. She said, "Woman of God, the doctor called me and said I have to come in right away because I have to undergo emergency surgery because they found a tumor on my spine." A couple of days after she got this surgery done, the spine fluid was gathering up behind her neck she had a big swelling there. She sent me a picture. She said, "Woman of God, you'll have to pray because the doctor said I may have to do another surgery to correct it." I said to her God didn't tell me that, so I prayed with her. The next day she called me. She said they didn't have to do another surgery because the spine fluid would go right back where it should go. She was happy. About two weeks after, she sent me a picture of her wiggling her toes for the first time in four-and-a-half years. She was very happy, and I was very happy because God did just what he said he would do. She started doing therapy for a while. She would send me videos of her doing her therapy. After a year in therapy, she started to walk very well again. She came back to the Bahamas after a while, and now she is doing two jobs. She is fine. God healed her.

Prayer works with faith. She is a happy woman now. She is writing her book, and she told me I am a part of her book. When we pray to God, we shouldn't have doubts. Our God is a big God, and if he said he will do it, he will do it. We have to have a close relationship with God. When we have a close relationship with God, he speaks to us himself. We don't have to go to others to get confirmation unless he sends someone with confirmation.

Every child of God should have a close relationship with him. I have so many testimonies about what God has done in the lives of the people I prayed for. I am only a vessel that the Lord chose to use because I made myself available for him to use. He said in John 12:32, "If I be lifted up from the earth, I will draw all men close to me."

All we have to do is to lift Jesus up. We have to lift him up high because he deserves all the praise, all the glory, and all the honor. My God is a healer. We just need to trust him. He said in Psalm 107:20, "He sent his word and healed them and delivered them from their destructions."

One morning as I was in prayer, the Lord gave me a phone number to call. When I called the number, a little boy answered the phone. I asked him whose phone he was using. He said his mother's. I told him to give the phone to his mother, and so he did.

I said to the mother, "Good morning, ma'am. I don't know you, but the Lord asked me to pray with you. I don't know what your needs are today for prayer, but God dropped your number in my spirit to call you."

She said to me, "I have breast cancer."

I replied, "You are healed in the name of Jesus. You are healed in the mighty name of Jesus. I command healing over you right now in the name of Jesus."

She then said, "I know I am a woman of God; I know I am healed. God is on time. God is never late. He is always on time."

Her faith and my faith were very strong in God. God used me so mightily in the healing ministry. I just had to speak a word in someone's life, and the Lord would bring it to pass. I have seen God do so many miracles. Now I am a faith walker, and I know nothing is too big for my God. God is an awesome God. We just need to trust him. Trust the process. He will come through for us if we believe. This woman couldn't stop praising the Lord.

One day my sister told me she went to the doctor to do her pap smear and the doctor told her they found out she had cancer. I told her, "On your way to work, stop by me so I could pray with you." She stopped by my house before she went to work. I anointed her stomach with olive oil and kept saying, "Not today, not today, not today, not today." I rebuked everything that was not of God against this woman of God, and I prayed in the name of Jesus. I told that cancer to dry up, rendered it powerless, and called it null and void in the name of Jesus. After she left the house, the Holy Spirit spoke to me and told me to tell her to get avocado leaves and cucumber leaves. She was to boil it and drink it. I called her and told her what the spirit told me, and she said okay. She had to undergo a follow-up biopsy to see what type of cancer it was. She called her doctor to say she was going to try the bush, so the doctor told her instead of coming in two weeks to do the biopsy, she could take a month and see what would happen. She told the doctor she was going to pray about it. After a month she went to do her biopsy, and she sent me a text from the doctor's office. She was negative for cancer.

Nothing in this world can make me doubt my God. God is awesome. I give him all the praise, all the glory, and all the honor. He is a promise keeper. We only have to believe. You see, the name of Jesus is a powerful name; there is power in the name of Jesus. The Bible tells us in Philippians 2:10–11, "That at the name of Jesus every knee should bow, of those in heaven and of those on earth and of those under the earth, and that every tongue should confess that Jesus Christ is Lord to the glory of God the Father."

So I know when I pray in the name of Jesus, every sickness and every disease got to bow. Jeremiah 29:11 says, "I know the plans I have for you, declares the Lord, plans to prosper you and not to harm you, plans to give you hope and a future." God did not tell us we wouldn't go through pain, sickness, and disease. He takes care of his children. Psalm 34:19 says, "The righteous person may have many troubles but the Lord delivers him from them all."

He did not say he would deliver us from some of the troubles; he said he'd deliver us from them all. We have to believe God's Word over our lives. He said we will have many troubles—many troubles, not just some, not just one, not just two, but many troubles—but if we trust him and believe in him, he will deliver us out of them all. What an awesome God we serve. This man I met called Jesus is the Son of the living God, my Father who art in heaven.

One morning my church sister called me and said her sugar level and her blood pressure were very high. She said she was eating right and taking her medication but with no success. I prayed with her. And after we finished praying, I said to her, "Go and test your pressure and your sugar right now and let me know if they went down." She called back in an hour and said her sugar level and her blood pressure were normal. We prayed with faith, knowing that God would answer our prayers.

I have seen God do so many miracles. God uses me in a mighty way to perform his wonders. God is a God of order. If he said so, he will do it. My life depends on God. I cannot do anything without him. I am nothing without him. I am a vessel that God chooses to use. I will always make myself available for God to use me. It is a good feeling to be used by the Almighty God, the all-powerful God, the omnipotent God, the omnipresent God, the omnificent God. Oh, how I love him. I cannot explain my love for God. *Love* is an action word, so to show God I love him, I have to do the things that he called me to do.

I came from a life of abuse, rape, molestation, depression, and pain to a life of peace, tranquility, joy, and love. It was worth it. My life is filled with the peace of God, the peace that only comes from God. The world doesn't have that peace; the world cannot give that peace. I have a very close relationship with God.

I remember one morning I was walking to work and he said to me, "Repent before you come into my presence." I thank God for the Holy Spirit, the spirit of the true and living God, the spirit that always quickens me. If I say anything wrong, the spirit will let me know to go and apologize or to repent. The spirit of God is very active in my life. There's nothing I can do without the Holy Spirit. Thank God for his Holy Spirit, the spirit of truth that leads us and directs us into all truth. We have to listen to the true spirit of God. He said in his Word that his sheep know his voice, so if we are children of God, we should know his voice.

I remember one morning I was lying down in my bed. I was in between being asleep and awake, and this man came over me and anointed me on my forehead. He said to me, "You are sealed." God is such an awesome God.

I remember one day I was so upset about something that happened, and while I was in the kitchen cooking, I was talking to the Lord about it in my spirit. He said I was a trailblazer. God will comfort us in the midst of the storm in our lives. My anchor holds firm in Christ because he promised me in Deuteronomy 31:6, "Be strong and courageous; do not be afraid or terrified because of them for the Lord your God is with you; he will never leave you nor forsake you."

So I have to hold on to the promises of God. His Word is strong and powerful. God speaks to me so many times in dreams and visions. I thank God that he chooses me. I thank him for looking beyond my flaws. I am now living my life totally depending on God to direct me, to lead me where he wants me to go. He told me in Psalm 37:23, "The steps of a good man are ordered by the Lord and he delights in his way." And David said in Psalm 37:25, "I have been young and now am old yet have I not seen the righteous forsaken nor his seed begging bread." God will always take care of his people. God keeps his promises toward us. We fail him, but he never fails us.

I remember one morning as I was in prayer, he spoke to me and said, "You are under an open heaven. A minister is going to die suddenly." A week later a minister in Jamaica was in a crash and died suddenly. I was in America when he spoke to me about it. It's amazing how God uses his people. God could speak to us anywhere as long as we position ourselves to hear from him.

I remember, when it was time for the election in the United States, I was praying and asked God who was going to be the next president. I was praying about it for a while. When I was home lying in my bed, the spirit said to me, "It's gonna be a flip in the script." President Biden *won* the election against Donald Trump. God has been so faithful to me. He never let me down. I pray for so many people, and they get their healing.

A gentleman one time called me from all the way in Jamaica and said to me he had a sore on his ankle for a while and it was so bad. He sent me pictures of his foot swollen. He couldn't sleep in the night. He was in so much pain. I prayed with him and told him I had given his foot three weeks to dry up in the name of Jesus. After I finished praying, the spirit said to me to tell him to use the Jack Hanna Bush on his foot, so I did. Three weeks after, he sent me pictures of his foot, and the sore was drying up. After a while his foot was healed.

God is a good God. I am using the gift that God gave to me to heal and to deliver people. Healing comes from God, not from man. It is God who does the healing. I pray in faith knowing that God will answer my prayer. Our prayers are not always answered the way we want them answered. If it's God's will, he will bring it to pass. We only have to believe; all things are possible with God.

Unemployed people will call me, and I will pray with them. They will call back to say they got the job. I will pray with people for their marriages and their finances, and God answers and turns their situation around.

I watch God move so many times in so many ways. He tells us in Luke 10:19, "I have given you authority to trample on snakes and scorpions and to overcome all the power of the enemy; nothing will harm you." So I know I got power through Jesus Christ over the enemy. We have to remember we are not weak Christians. We got power through Jesus Christ. Proverbs 18:21 says, "Death and life are in the power of the tongue and they that love it shall eat the fruit thereof."

So I always speak life. I know that I have power to speak things into existence, so I always speak life. I speak life into every dead situation. My Bible tells me in Numbers 23:19, "God is not a man that he should lie, neither the son of man, that he should repent. Hath he said, and shall he not do it? Or hath he spoken, and shall he not make it good?"

God speaks to his people in dreams and in visions. Job 33:15 says, "In a dream, in a vision of the night when deep sleep falls upon men while slumbering on their bed."

I am a happy person since I met Christ. I cannot describe the inner peace he gave me. I cannot find that peace anywhere but in Christ Jesus. Psalm 28:8 says, "The Lord is their strength and he is the saving strength of his anointed one." 2 Corinthians 12:9 says, "But he said to me, 'My grace is sufficient for you for my power is made perfect in weakness.' Therefore I will boast all the more gladly of my weaknesses so that the power of Christ may rest upon me."

I thank God for his strength. He is the reason I breathe. He is my first love. I give God thanks for not allowing the enemy to take me out in my sinful life. I give God thanks for drawing me closer to him. He sees my heart, and he knows I love him, so he draws me closer and closer and closer to him. There is no repentance in the grave. I could have died during the abuse, but he kept me for a purpose. He kept me for this set time, and the set time is now. He kept me so I could tell my story. He kept me so I could make a boast of him. He kept me so I could tell the world about him.

One morning while I was in prayer, he spoke to me. He said, "You are my glory carrier. I placed my glory upon you. Everywhere you go you will display my glory." It is not my glory but his glory. I am his glory carrier. He also said to me, "I placed the Elijah mantle on you. You are a recipient in heaven." The following Sunday I went to church, and the pastor said, "Some of you in this church are glory carriers, and you all aren't even aware of it." So I knew right away it was confirmation for me.

Also, that very Sunday in church while I was worshiping, a lady sitting in the front came and hugged me. She said, "You have an anointing on you. I feel the fire from up in the front." Another lady came and hugged me, and she said, "You made a difference in church today." So I know that God's Word cannot lie. He confirms his Word. God will send someone with a word for you.

Sometimes I will be talking to God about something that happened, and he will drop in my spirit to go and read the Bible. He will wake me up in the morning time and give me a scripture to read. God is so awesome. God is amazing. When you have a close relationship with God, you can never go wrong.

I love to tell people about the goodness of God because I know what he did for me, he can also do it for you. I want my book to inspire people, especially those who were and are still being abused and raped, those who are hooked on drugs, those who are molested, those who are hurting, those who are in bondage, those who are on the verge of committing suicide, and those who are battered and bruised. I want them to know that they can make it; they will make it. With God all things are possible. Ephesians 3:20–21 says, "Now unto to him that is able to do exceedingly abundantly above all that we ask or think according to the power that worketh in us, unto him be glory in the church by Christ Jesus throughout all ages, world without end." Amen.

I want my book to change people's lives. I want my book to inspire people. I want them to see that there is a better life. But we have to seek him with all our heart, all our body, all our spirit, and all our soul. We have to seek him. We have to want him from deep inside. He said in Jeremiah 29:13, "You will seek me and find me when you search for me with all your heart."

We have to put God first. We have to give up on the things of the world and seek God first. I got so much hurt in my life from just being in the world, not paying attention to the things of God.

There is nothing in this world for me but sin, shame, and disgrace. The most peaceful time I've had in my entire life is when I found Christ. All I want is him. All I want is God.

I can't get enough of him. Nothing in this world entices me anymore, only the things of God. I am chasing after the things of God. All I want to hear is "Well done, my good and faithful servant." Now that you've read my story, you can learn from my story—what I went through when I was in the world and what I achieved when I started to serve Christ in spirit and truth and in the very beauty of holiness.

I am now waiting on Christ Jesus because he said in Revelation 22:12, "And behold I come quickly and my reward is with me to give every man according as his work shall be." Thank God for Jesus. Thank God for giving us his one and only Son, Jesus Christ, who died for our sins.

What a love our Father displays to his children. John 15:13 says, "Greater love hath no man than this, that a man lay down his life for his friend." Psalm 119:105 says, "That word is a lamp unto my feet, a light unto my path." God's Word cannot lie. His Word is a lamp unto our feet and a light unto our path. Without God's word we are in darkness, and when we walk in darkness, we stumble and fall.

Because I am standing on his Word now, I can love my neighbor as I love myself. Even if they offend me, I can still love them, I can forgive them, and I can move on because I am walking in the light and not in the darkness. Life becomes lighter and brighter.

2 Corinthians 3:17 says, "Therefore if any man be in Christ, he is new creature. Old things are passed away; behold all things are become new." Even though we live in the world, we are not part of the world.

The Bible tells us in John 4:23–24, "But the hour is coming and now is when the true worshippers will worship the Father in spirit and truth for the Father is seeking such to worship him." God is a spirit, and those who worship him must worship in spirit and truth. God is looking for true worshippers.

He told us in Revelation 3:16 (KJV), "So then because thou art lukewarm and neither hot nor cold, I will spue thee out of my mouth." God is looking for true worshippers who are going to worship him in spirit and in truth and in the very beauty of holiness.

Sometimes we get hurt in life, and we spend the rest of our life living defeated. We don't have to live defeated. Because of the blood of Jesus, we are not defeated. We are conquerors through Christ Jesus. We are warriors through Christ Jesus. We don't have to sit back and be defeated. Mark 10:46–53 (KJV) tells us about the story of the blind beggar Bartimaeus:

> And they came to Jericho and as he went out of Jericho with his disciples and a great number of people, blind Bartimaeus, the son of Timaeus, sat by the highway side begging. And when he heard that it was Jesus of Nazareth, he began to cry out and say, "Jesus, thou son of David, have mercy on me." And many charged him that he should hold his peace but he cried the more a great deal, "Thou son of David have mercy on me." And Jesus stood still and commanded him to be called and they call the blind man saying unto him, "Be of good comfort. Rise. He called thee." And he casting away his garment rose and came to Jesus. And Jesus answered and said unto him, "What will thou that I should do unto thee?" The blind man said unto him, "Lord, that I might receive my sight." And Jesus said unto him, "Go thy way; thy faith hath made thee whole." And immediately he received his sight and followed Jesus in the way.

You see, Bartimaeus could have stopped shouting, but he was trying to get Jesus's attention. Even though the people were trying to shut him up, he was still shouting. See, sometimes when we need Jesus's attention, we have to keep calling on Jesus. We have to continue seeking him until we find him.

Bartimaeus did not give up even though the crowd was trying to shut him up. That was a cry of desperation. That was a cry for help. And with that one encounter with Jesus, Bartimaeus's eyes were opened, and he followed Jesus. He never turned back. He continued to follow Jesus.

Some of us have similar situations. Our eyes may not be naturally blind like Bartimaeus, but our eyes are spiritually blind. Our ears are spiritually deaf, so we have to call out with a cry of desperation. Jesus is never too busy to not hear our cry.

Bartimaeus's whole life was changed at that moment. He didn't have to sit and beg anymore. He didn't need that coat anymore. He didn't need that stick anymore, because he had an encounter with Jesus. One encounter with Jesus can change our lives. Bartimaeus didn't let the crowd stop him from shouting. What an experience. What an encounter. His life was never the same. He didn't sit down. He followed Jesus.

We can learn from that story that we cannot let anyone stop us from crying out to Jesus. We have to totally surrender to God. We have to pray without ceasing. We have to stay on our knees. We cannot give the enemy any loophole. We have to learn to forgive one another and love one another with the love of Christ. Many times, our prayers are not answered because we hold on to unforgiveness. It is like poison. We cannot hold on to unforgiveness.

I learned to forgive everyone who hurt me, even after a few years of being saved. God allowed my father to come back in my life so that I could forgive him, so that I could let go of everything I was carrying around. God even used me to pray for my dad on his sickbed. Even after so many years, when I heard from my dad, he was still the same man I met as a child. Nothing really changed about him.

But you see, something was changed with me. I was not the same little girl back then. This time I knew who I was. This time I knew whom God called me to be. This time I was much stronger and wiser. This time God had already prepared me spiritually. So, when my dad came back around, I forgave him, because when I go in the presence of Abba Father, I want to be clean. I am not perfect, but I am striving for perfection. I forgave my dad for the molestation.

One night I was in prayer, and there was a love that came over me for him. I got his number from someone. I was fifty and reconciling with my father after what he had done to me. I even started sending him money for his medication. He told me he had prostate cancer and he was in the hospital, and I prayed for him while he was in the hospital. He said to me over the phone, "My daughter, I cannot see you, but I can feel you." He wasn't feeling me; he was feeling the Holy Spirit. He called me back the next day and said, "You are a real woman of God." He said the doctor hooked him up seven times to do surgery, but he didn't know what happened after I finished praying. Two weeks after he called me, he told me the doctor said the cancer had been healed and he only had a swollen prostate and that there was no cancer.

God will use us mightily if we surrender the hurt and all the pain. After all that I went through with my dad, God still used me to pray for him, and he got his healing. After we reconciled and after his healing, he would still ask me for money. I would still send him money. If I didn't get to the phone and answer in time, my sister in Jamaica told me he would talk about me badly and say things like "I don't know about this woman. She called me to reconcile, and now that I am calling her, she's not answering." Sometimes when he called me and I was not close to my phone, he would get angry. All he ever wanted from me was money, money, and more money. If I didn't have any money, he would get mad.

One day over the phone I had to remind him that he molested me and I had forgiven him. His response to me was "If I catch you close, I would headshot you." I began to cry at these words, because I could not believe that he said them. You see, he got mad because he was only using me for money and that was his only reason for reconciling.

But I thank God that I forgave him, and now I am the one who has peace. I thank God that he allowed me to forgive my father because he was the only one whom I held in my heart, and Lord knows it was hard for me to forgive him. But with the strength of Almighty God, I did it. Thank God I did forgive, because we didn't speak after that time until he passed away. But I had peace, because the Lord led me to forgive him fully.

See, what happened is I truly had love in my heart for him. But he didn't love me, nor did he love my brothers. Maybe he did not know how to love.

One of my brothers passed away, and my dad didn't even know he died. But God had given me the healing gift. That's why I was able to pray for his healing. The last thing my dad said to me was that if he caught me in Jamaica, he would headshot me. That was not nice for a dad to say to his child, especially a child whom he molested at such a young age.

But I thank God for Jesus Christ who died on the cross for my sins and gave me a second chance to life. I thank God for not taking me in my sins. I thank God for drawing me closer to him. Forgiveness is the key. We have to forgive.

I felt sorry for my dad after I got saved because I knew he allowed the enemy to use him all his life. I felt sorry for him because he didn't know who Christ was. When I told him about God, he would tell me, "I don't go to church. Only hypocrites are in church." So I knew I had to forgive him.

We have to forgive people because it's not the person who hurt us but it's the devil whom they allow to use them. I forgave my father. I forgave everyone who hurt me. I am sorry for these people. I feel sorry for them. I feel very sorry for them because I know they allow the enemy to use them.

My children's dad apologized to me. He told my children I was the best woman to ever walk into his life and he was sorry for the way he treated me. He apologized, and I told him I forgave him.

I cannot let anything stop me from running this race. I have to finish the race that I started for Christ. He equips me with the equipment that I need to run the race—patience, love, kindness, forgiveness, joy, peace, and humility. I thank God I do not look like what I've been through. I am a minister, I am an intercessor, and I am a prayer warrior. I am also writing my book, so I cannot hold on to the past, as it's too much for me to deal with in the present.

So I let the past go. It is now in God's hands. I am now a happy person. So I want my book to inspire people. I want them to read my story and find joy. I want to let them know that if I did it, they could do it too. Just trust in God, put him first, and let him be the number one priority.

God is love. He first loved me, so I have no other choice but to love him. He looks beyond my faults, and he still loves me. What an awesome God we serve. When I am home, God will put a song in my spirit. I will sing. I will praise him. Or he will send me to his Word to read a chapter or a verse. Sometimes he will allow someone to call me with a good message or someone to send me a message on the phone. I love him so much.

Philippians 4:7 (KJV) says, "And the peace that surpasses all understanding will guard your heart and mind in Christ Jesus." Do not be anxious about anything. Tell your request to God with thanksgiving. If we keep our mind on him, he will give us that peace that surpasses all understanding that will guard our heart and mind.

I always find myself praying in my spirit. If I am walking, I am praying in my spirit or singing in my spirit. My spirit always has a prayer or a song. I keep my mind on Jesus, this man I met who changed my life forever. Jesus died on the cross for me so that I could get forgiveness of all my sins, and his blood washed me and cleansed me of all unrighteousness. Thank God for Jesus Christ, his one and only Son. God said he loves us, and he shows us his love. *Love* is an action word. God displays that love for us by sending his one and only Son, Jesus Christ, to die on Calvary's cross for our sins. What a love.

I have no other choice but to love the Father, Son, and Holy Spirit. My story has a rough start but a happy ending. Thank God for his Son, Jesus Christ, the man I met who changed my life forever.

We cannot hold on to grudge; we have to let it go.

When I pray, I ask God to let his perfect will be done in my life, not my way nor my will. I know that God knows what is best for me. It's not about me; it's all about God. I wouldn't trade my relationship with God for anything in this world. Nothing in this world is valuable to me because when I put him first, he takes care of everything attached to me—my children, my grandchildren, my finances, my home, my jobs. Everything around me is taken care of—my family, my friends, my neighbors. God takes care of everything attached to me.

I pray that my story will change lives. All I want to hear is "Well done, my good and faithful servant." My brothers and sisters, hold on to Jesus. Let God use you. There is a deeper depth in Christ Jesus. Keep on praying, keep on fasting, and keep on trusting. He will take you higher in the supernatural. Build a relationship with the Father. Spend time in the Word. Spend quality time in the presence of God.

Whatever situation we go through, he will deliver us from, every hurt and every pain. Seek him today while he may be found. It is a great feeling to be used by the all-powerful God. It's a great feeling to be used by the Almighty God. It is priceless, my brothers and sisters. I pray this book will change your life forever as you read it. I wrote this book out of love because I know there's someone out there who is going through something that needs an encounter with Jesus Christ.

Whatever we go through in life, God could turn it around for good for us who love him and are called by his name. There is a scripture that touched me deep inside. Psalm 139:8 (KJV) says, "If I ascend up into heaven, thou art there. If I make my bed in hell, behold you are there."

My brothers and sisters in Christ, there is no place we could go out of the presence of Almighty God. He is omnipresent, he is omniscient, and he is omnipotent. God he is here, and he is everywhere. What a mighty God we serve. What an awesome God we serve. Who wouldn't love him? Who wouldn't want to serve him? I pray that my book will change someone's life for the better. My story brings glory to the Almighty God. He gets the glory out of my story. *All glory, all honor, and all praise belong to God.*

> Our Father who art in heaven, hallowed be thy name. Thy kingdom come. Thy will be done on earth as it is in heaven. Give us this day our daily bread and forgive us our trespasses as we forgive those that trespass against us and lead us not into temptation but deliver us from evil for

thine is the kingdom, the power, and the glory forever and ever. Amen.

The LORD is my shepherd; I shall not want. He maketh me to lie down in green pastures: he leadeth me beside the still waters. He restoreth my soul: he leadeth me in the paths of righteousness for his name's sake. Yea, though I walk through the valley of the shadow of death, I will fear no evil: for thou art with me; thy rod and thy staff they comfort me. Thou preparest a table before me in the presence of mine enemies: thou anointest my head with oil; my cup runneth over. Surely goodness and mercy shall follow me all the days of my life: and I will dwell in the house of the LORD for ever. (Psalm 23:1–6 KJV)